EFT (Emotional Freedom Techniques)
for Children

Anne Unsworth

AuthorHouse™ UK Ltd.
500 Avebury Boulevard
Central Milton Keynes, MK9 2BE
www.authorhouse.co.uk
Phone: 08001974150

© 2009 Anne Unsworth. All rights reserved.

No part of this book may be reproduced, stored in a retrieval system, or transmitted by any means without the written permission of the author.

First published by AuthorHouse 7/21/2009

ISBN: 978-1-4389-7094-3 (sc)

This book is printed on acid-free paper.

Contents

Introduction..3
You are Energy!...5
I can feel my Energy!..6
How can you fix it?..8
The Happy Tappy Buttons...10
Your "Yum-Yuck" card...19
The Happy Tappy Points...21
The BIG Blocks ~...22
    1. Anger..22
    2. Worry...26
    3. Fear..30
    4. I'm Not Good Enough!..34
    5. Sadness...38
    6. Guilt...42

Introduction.

During the past few years schools have attempted to encourage emotional literacy amongst children.

This is an admirable step but as a former teacher I feel that it does not go far enough.

The advent of such therapies as Emotional Freedom Techniques is the next logical step in the process of awakening children to the realisation that they do have control over their actions and reactions in many situations.

This book is designed for use by teachers who have had an introduction to EFT and, with consistency, it will prove to be a useful tool to enable pupils to clear away their emotional debris and be ready to learn.

While recognising that each case is individual, the general themes covered provide a starting point for further work.

I look forward to the day when all children are able to effectively handle their emotional wellbeing!

Anne Unsworth. B.A., AAMET,

You are Energy!

Your body is made up of energy, flowing round and round.

Some people call this energy "Chi" or "Ki".

It is just like electricity and it gives your body POWER.

The energy flows through invisible lines called MERIDIANS.

If the energy is flowing well and freely, you will feel well and happy.

I can feel my Energy!

You can't see your energy but here is a little experiment to help you to feel it.

- Rub your hands together very fast until they are warm.
- Next, hold your hands in front of you with the palms facing each other.
- Then begin to move your hands slowly apart and back near each other.
- Do this a few times until you can feel the energy like a ball in your hands.
- Play with your energy ball, moving it up and down, in and out.

This shows you your own energy. Just imagine how much energy is in your whole body if that little bit came from your hands!

BUT

Sometimes the energy gets stuck and it can't move freely.

Then you feel scared or sad or angry or even ill.

How can you fix it?

Look at this poem that tells you about the energy and later we will find out how to open up those lines of energy so that you can feel happy again.

Inside my body energy flows
Where it comes from, nobody knows
When it gets stuck, I always feel down
From the tips of my toes right up to my crown.

But now I know just what I can do
If you join in you can learn it too
I tap on the points that set it free
And then I feel yum, That's the key!

Now we need to learn how to tap on the points to set the blocked energy free.

We call these points **"The Happy Tappy Buttons"**

Let's find out where they are and how to use them.

The Happy Tappy Buttons

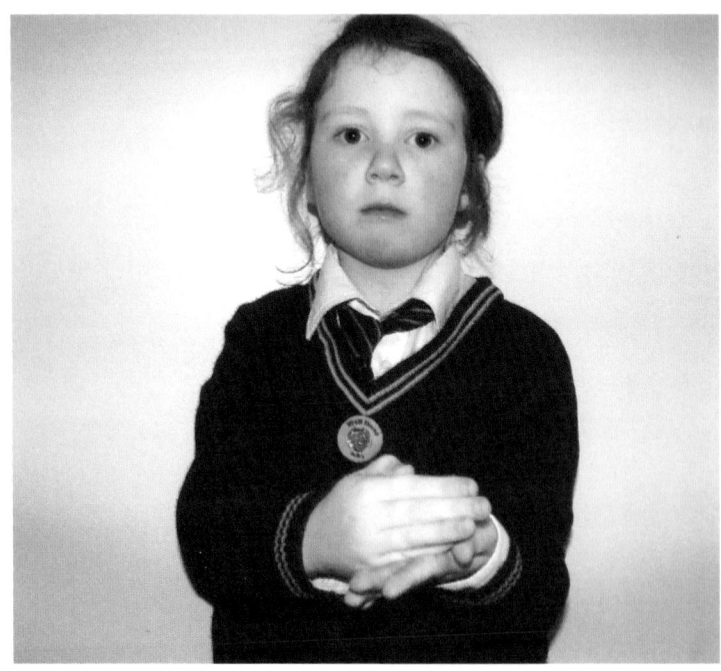

The Karate Chop.

When you have a problem the first thing to do is to set it up to be karate chopped. This is on the part of your hand that you would use to karate chop something. Tap this part of your hand while you set your problem up. This is the Set-up.

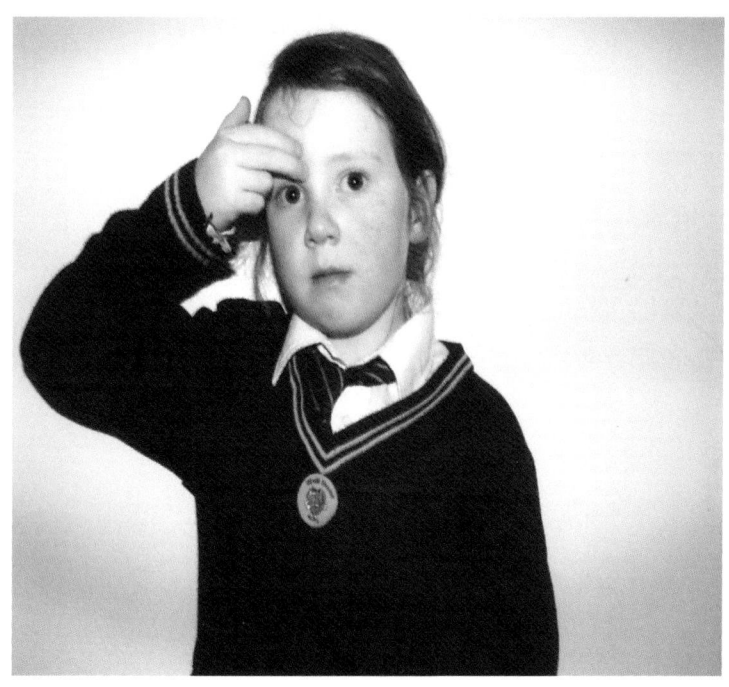

The Eyebrow.

This is right at the start of your eyebrow.

The Side Brow.

On this one you tap at the outside edge of your eyebrow.

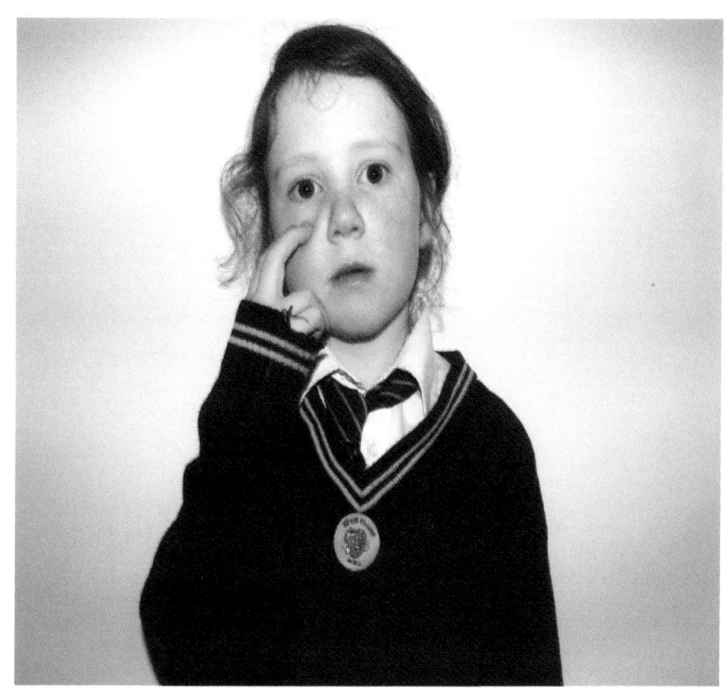

The High Cheek.

This is on the bone just below your eye.

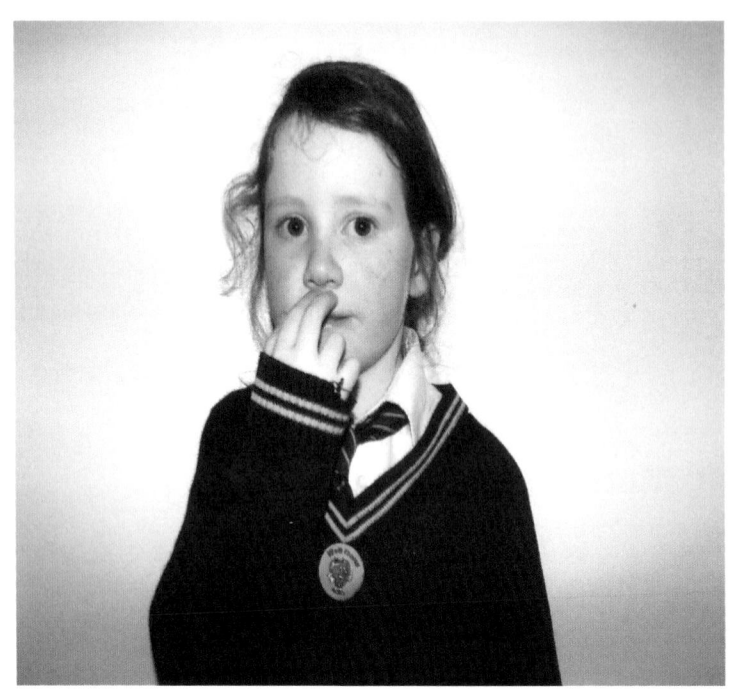

The Nose.

This one is just below your nose and above your top lip.

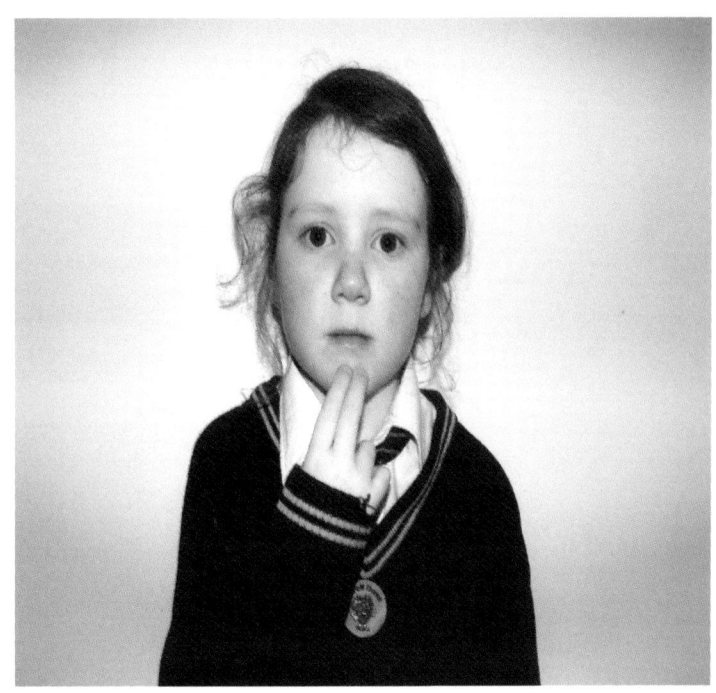

The Chin

Now you are tapping between your chin and your bottom lip.

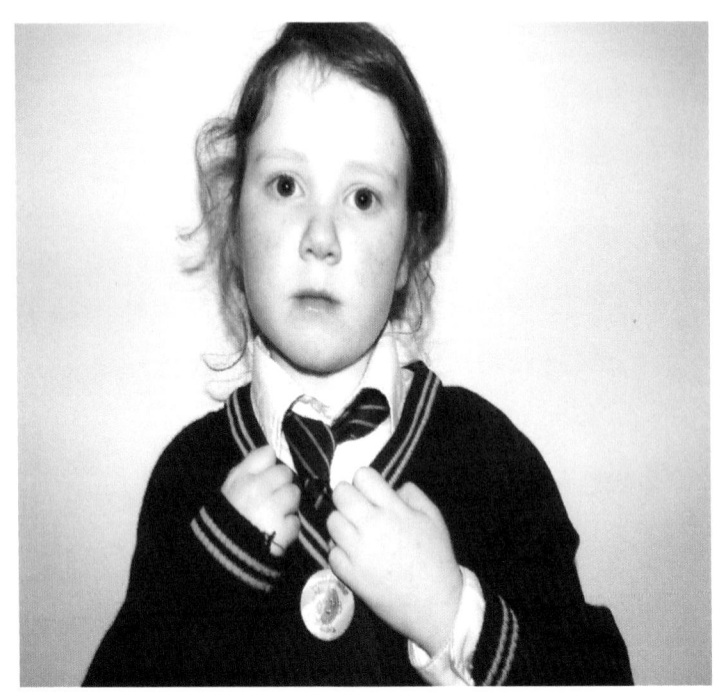

Tarzan.

This one is fun to do. Just thump your chest like Tarzan!

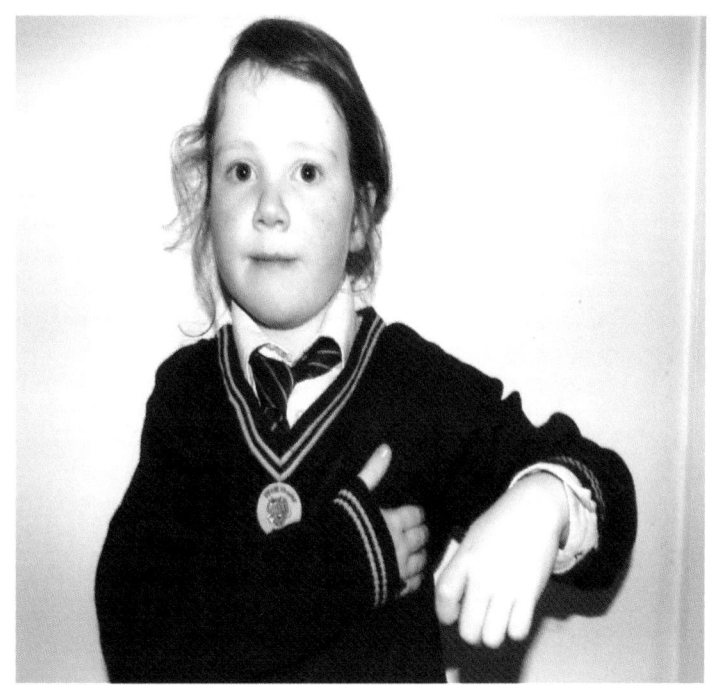

The Monkey.

This one is fun too. Tap under your arm like a monkey.

The Big Top

The last one is right on top of your head. It's like the Big Top of the circus tent and it is the place where you put your happy thoughts at the end of your tapping rounds.

Your *"Yum-Yuck"* card.

You will know when your energy is not flowing well because you will feel sad or angry or upset or just "yuck".

To help you to show how you feel, you can make a "yum-yuck" card like the one shown.

You can move the pointer to the section of the card that shows how you are feeling right now about your problem.

Your first exercise.

- ✓ Close your eyes and let your mind travel round your body.
- ✓ Is there anywhere that you think there might be a block in the energy?
- ✓ Now decide how much of the energy is being blocked. If it's really bad, it will be yuck, If it's no problem, it's yum.
- ✓ Show that on your card.
- ✓ Next put the card down and let's decide how to say what the problem is.
- ✓ Even though you have this problem, it's just an energy block and you are still the same great person you have always been.
- ✓ Set these words up for a karate chop.
- ✓ So we begin by saying "Even though I feel………………… I am still a great person and I'm ok.

Your "Yum/Yuck" card.

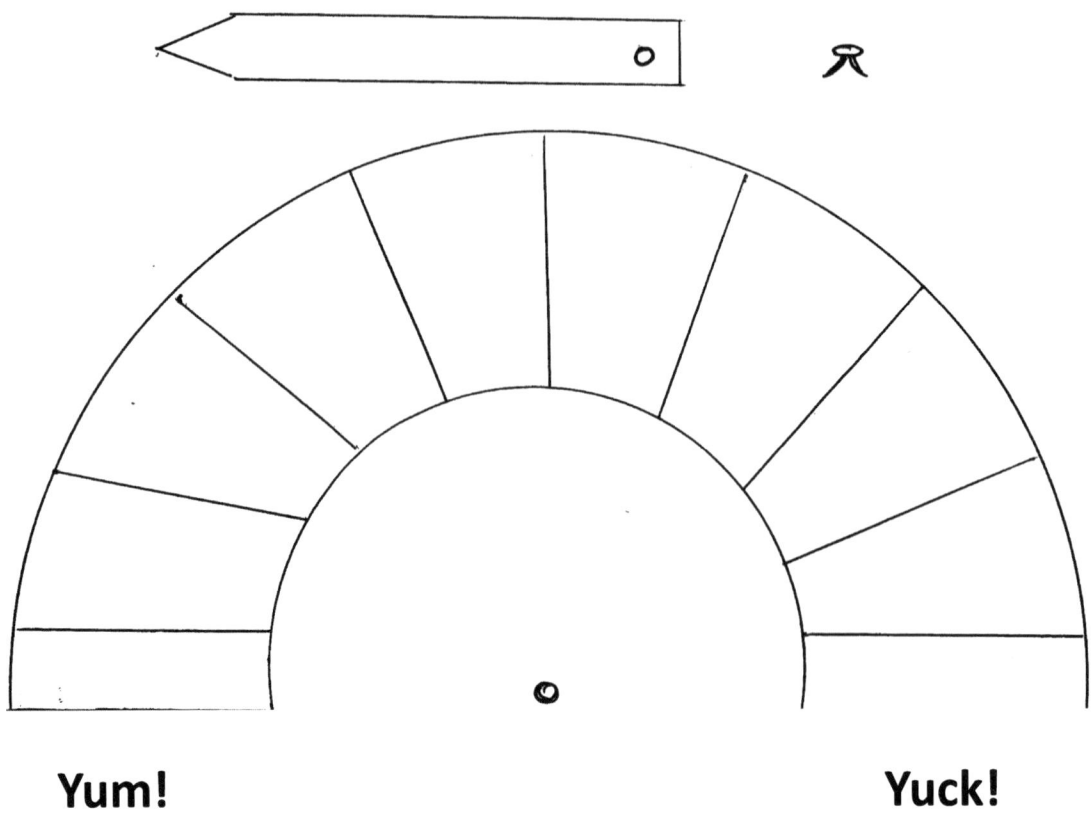

Yum! **Yuck!**

You can copy this shape onto card and cut it out.

Join the pointer to the card with a split pin. You can colour your card if you want to. Put your favourite colour on the Yum side and a colour you are not so keen on at the Yuck side.

Now you are ready to use it.

The Happy Tappy Points.

- ➢ **Eyebrow.** Tap 5 or 6 times on the part of your eyebrow nearest to your nose and say "I feel ...."
- ➢ **Side brow.** Tap 5 or 6 times on the outside edge of your eyebrow and say "I feel............................"
- ➢ **High Cheek.** Do the same again on the bone at the top of your cheek and say again "I feel........................."
- ➢ **Under Nose.** Do the same again
- ➢ **Chin.** Same again
- ➢ **Tarzan.** Same again
- ➢ **Monkey.** Same again
- ➢ **Big Top.** Same again

It's easy, isn't it?

That's one round completed. If there is still some blocking going on, just do the whole round again but this time say "Even though I still feel a bit of this .... it's just some blocked energy and I'm still a great person."

Then when you tap the Happy Tappy Buttons say "This bit of ...."

The BIG Blocks ~
1. Anger.

Sometimes we get great big blocks in our energy.
One of the biggest blocks is when we are angry.
Lots of things or people can make us feel angry.

What things or people make YOU angry?

You might say something like:
- "I get angry when my friend won't play with me."

    Or

- "I feel mad when I don't get my own way."
- "I am cross when I have to get up in the morning."
- "Nobody listens to me!"
- "I'm cross because it's not fair that.........."

Everybody gets angry sometimes!

How does Anger make you feel?

23

What can you feel happening in your body when you are angry? What do you do?

- Do you burn up with rage?
- Do you scream and shout?
- Do you run away and hide?
- Do you feel ugly inside and out?
- Do you feel as if all of you is stuck inside your head?

These are NOT good feelings. You wouldn't want to always feel like this, would you?

Well, you don't have to!
Now you have a choice!

Remember that anger creates a big block in your energy. And big blocks stop you being happy.

Let's laser this anger!

Laser the ANGER!

First of all use your "Yum/Yuck" card to show how strong your anger is right now.

Now we need to set up our self talk on the Karate chop.

"Even though I feel really angry because……………………………… and I could cry/scream/shout, I am still a great person and I'm ready to put this anger down."

Say this 3 times while tapping on the Karate chop.

Now begin to tap the Happy Tappy Buttons as you say,

"This anger."

Start with the Eyebrow, then Side brow, High cheek, Nose, Chin, Tarzan, Monkey, and Big Top.

When you finish one round, go back to your "Yum/Yuck" card and show if the anger has moved down a bit.

If you were REALLY angry you might need to go round once more or even a few times more!

Just for fun, when the anger has gone, try to get mad about the same thing. Bet you can't!

The BIG Blocks~
2. Worry.

What would it be like if you never had to worry?

EVERYBODY worries about things. Some people worry a lot but others don't seem to worry much at all.

Do you worry a lot or a little? What do you worry about?

Have you ever known a time when worrying made something better?

The problem is that even though we know that worrying never helps, we still do it!

Wouldn't it be great if we could stop ourselves right at the beginning of our worrying?

Guess what! WE CAN!

Wave the worry Goodbye!

As before, think about a big worry that you have.

Give it a level on your "Yum/Yuck" card.

Remember to keep that worry in your head while we work it out.

Next set up your self- talk on the Karate chop.

"Even though I am worried sick that .... I know that my worrying will make no difference to what happens and I want to free my energy flow and put this worry away. I am still a great person and I am already free."

Now tap on each of the Happy Tappy Buttons and say

"This worry."

Some tricks to learn.

Because worries can be very big we can try another trick to send the worry on its way.

As you go round the Tappy Buttons a second time, put different words about the worry on each one, like this......

Eyebrow ~ "This really big worry"

Side brow ~ "It's too heavy for me to carry."

High Cheek ~ "I'm ready to leave it behind."

Nose ~ "I know things will work out anyway."

Chin~ "I have no need to worry about this."

Tarzan ~ "Somebody else can do the worrying if they want."

Monkey ~ "I've finished with it."

Big Top ~ "Now I choose to be free."

Now, show on your "Yum/Yuck" card how you feel about that old worry.

The BIG blocks ~
3. Fear.

Fear is a bit like a big worry.

We are all afraid sometimes. We can have really BIG fears or our fears can be quite small. We don't need to carry fear around because it blocks our energy.

What are you afraid of?

You might be afraid of the dark or afraid of dogs or spiders or another animal. You might be afraid that you or someone in your family will be poorly. Some people are afraid of new situations or of meeting someone they don't know.

There are hundreds of things we could be afraid of if we really think about it.

But why be afraid when we can do something about it?

Fade the Fear!

- First of all, think about the fear you want to fade.
- Next we set it up on the karate chopping block.
- On the karate chop we might say something like............... "Even though I have this fear of .... I am still a great person and I really like myself."
- Say this 3 times while tapping the karate chop point.
- Now work your way around all the Happy Tappy Buttons saying on each "This fear."
- When you get round once, have another look at the fear and see if it has faded a bit.
- If it has, go round again until you don't feel afraid of that same thing any more.
- If your fear is still as big as ever, you can try the tricks you learned in the last chapter.
- On each Tappy Button you can say something about the fear like this......................

Tricks to Fade the Fear.

- "This big fat fear that keeps me awake at night"

- "This fear that is just blocking my energy"

- This fear about ...."

- I don't need to carry this fear any more"

- I have no more use for this fear"

- This fear that started when I ...."
- I choose to be free of this fear"

- I choose to be happy and free"

Always end at the Big Top with a happy statement.

The BIG blocks ~
4. I'm Not Good Enough!

How often have you felt as if you were not good enough?

Even grown-ups feel like this sometimes.

Maybe someone has made you feel not good enough, a friend, a parent, a teacher or someone else, or maybe you did it to yourself by imagining that you should be better than you are at certain things.

Think about a time when you felt like everybody was better than you. Did someone call you an unpleasant name? How did you feel inside? What happened in your body?

You probably didn't realise it at the time but you had just allowed a big block to stop your energy flowing freely.

The problem is that those blocks stay there until you tap them free. Let's do that now.

Free the Flow.

- Begin by calling to mind the biggest time when you felt not good enough. Think about who was there, why you weren't good enough, what was said and so on.

- Show on your "Yum/Yuck" card how strong the feeling is at this moment.

- Now think of a good way to describe that feeling for the karate chop block.

- You might say something like……………………………………………
"Even though I always feel as if I'm no good at Maths I know I'm still a great person and there is nobody like me in the whole world."

- Use words that fit how YOU feel rather than just following the words in the book.

- So, with the problem on the karate chop, remember to say it 3 times.

- Now you are ready to really free the flow!

- On each of the Happy Tappy Buttons you just need to say **"This not good enough feeling"**

- It is a good idea to go round again just to make sure before you examine the feeling again to see if it has come nearer to the "Yum" on your card

I AM good enough!

Feeling not good enough is a VERY BIG block so you may need to use the extra tricks again. Try this................................

- When you are putting the problem on the karate chop block, see if you can be really clear about what it was that made you feel not good enough.

- Use those exact words to describe the problem............... "Even though my friend said you're not very good at this game" or "Even though I tried my best but I still couldn't do it" or "Even though everybody else was able to swim a whole length and I couldn't"

- Remember to always finish the sentence with "I'm still a great person and I like myself or there's no-one else like me."

- Now, on the Happy Tappy Buttons you can put words from your problem like this...........................

- "I wasn't good enough, I tried my best, my friend said, I wanted to get it right, I am good at lots of things, there is no-one else quite like me, and so on.

- Make sure that you put something good on the Big Top!

The BIG Blocks~
5. Sadness.

Have you ever been really sad about something?

Things happen in our lives which make us feel so sad that we think we are all alone in our sadness. It doesn't have to be like this. Each day we have many choices to make and everything that happens allows us to make new choices.

Maybe you have felt sad because your friend wouldn't play or because you lost something or maybe you have had a BIG sadness like you feel when a person or a pet you knew has died.

Maybe we need to experience a bit of sadness sometimes so that we can appreciate the happiness.

If you knew that you could choose to be happy instead of sad, would you choose happiness?

Solve the Sadness Problem.

By now you will have a good idea of how to decide how strong the feeling is using your "Yum/Yuck card and how to set up your problem on the karate chop and to tap it down on the Happy Tappy Buttons. Here's a reminder.

- How strong is your sadness? Show it on your card.

- Think of a good way to describe your problem e.g
  "Even though I feel really sad that my cat died, I am still a great person and I love myself."
  Or

- "Even though I feel so sad that I could cry for a week and I don't even know why I feel this way, I am still a great person and I love myself."

- Set the problem up 3 times on the karate chop.

- Now work around the Happy Tappy Buttons saying, "This sadness."

- You might go round twice before you stop to see if the sadness has moved down nearer to "Yum".

- If you are a lot happier now, you can choose to stop but if you need to carry on then use the special tricks like this………
…………………………………….

Solve the Sadness Problem Even More.

- Start as you did before by working out how strong the sadness is now and showing it on your card.

- Set the sadness up on the karate chop using words that are meaningful to you.

- Say your set up statement 3 times.

- Next, put some of your statement words on to each of the Buttons as you tap.

- It might be something like this..
  Eyebrow: "I feel so sad"
  Side brow: "This sadness weighs me down."
  High cheek: "Nobody understands my sadness"
  Nose: "I wonder what it would be like to change this sadness into happiness."
  Chin: "Maybe it would be ok for me to leave the
  Tarzan: "I WILL leave the sadness behind.
  Monkey: " I choose to leave the sadness behind and I choose to be happy"
  Big Top: "I am happy and free."

- You can always go round again using the same or new words until you really do feel happy.

- When you finish it is a good idea to test your work by trying to feel the same way you did before about that same thing.

The BIG Blocks ~
6. Guilt.

Do you think there is anyone in the whole world that has never done anything wrong?

EVERYBODY has made a wrong choice at some time.

How you feel about that choice depends on what you do about it.

Maybe it is not something that you can put right very easily so it might be that you just end up feeling guilty because you knew better but still made the choice.

Do you have to hold on to and carry that guilt around with you for the rest of your life? NO, you don't!

Here's why.

Having you feel guilty does not help anyone else, even the person you made the wrong choice about.

All it does is BLOCK your ENERGY.

Gunning for Guilt.

So let's get that guilt out. You know how to check its strength and how to do the set-up and tapping by now. Here it is again.

- Decide how strong the guilt is and show that on your card.

- Decide how best to describe what your guilt feels like. It might be something like…………………………………………………………… It feels like a big heavy weight on my shoulders…………… or This guilty feeling makes me really uncomfortable….. or I feel bad in my chest because I did this……………………

- Choose whatever sounds most like the way you feel and use that as your set-up statement.

- "Even though I have this big heavy weight in my chest because I feel guilty that ……………………………….. I am still a great person and I still like/love myself."

- Say your set-up 3 times while tapping on the karate chop.

- For the first round you only need to say "This guilty feeling" on the Happy Tappy Buttons.

- When you have gone round twice, check how strong the feeling is now.

Tricks for Guilt.

Because guilt is usually quite strong, you will probably need to use the extra tricks to get it right down.

Remember that all you need to do is to put some of your words on each of the Tappy Buttons as you go round.

You can use the same set-up statement as before.

It might come out something like this……………………………………

- "Even though I am still feeling a bit guilty about …………. I know I was doing what I thought was best at the time and I love myself in spite of sometimes being wrong."
- Eyebrow:- "I made a wrong choice"
- Side brow:- "I am sorry for choosing the wrong thing"
- High cheek:-" I was doing what I had to at that time"
- Nose:- "I know how to make good choices"
- Chin:- "That time is past now and I choose to be free of that guilt"
- Tarzan:- "I am always improving"
- Monkey:- "I am able to see how my actions can affect other people"
- Big Top:- "I choose to be free and to allow other people to be free too."

EFT for Everything.

Well done! Now you know how to get rid of all those energy blocks.

We have read about and worked with ways to end fear, worry, guilt, sadness and not being good enough.

Now you are ready to really use your imagination!

You can use EFT for ANY problem, no matter how big or how small. It's the same routine for everything.

- Give your problem a level from 1-10.
- Set it up on the Karate Chop.
- Go round the Tappy Buttons saying the name of the problem.
- Go round again, just to make sure.
- Check the level again and if it's not gone use some of the extra tricks we tried before.

Happy Tapping!